# R

*Daily*

Catherine Upchurch

**LITURGICAL PRESS**
Collegeville, Minnesota

litpress.org

*Nihil Obstat:* Rev. Robert C. Harren, J.C.L., *Censor Librorum*

*Imprimatur:* ✠ Most Rev. Patrick M. Neary, C.S.C., Bishop of St. Cloud, July 22, 2024

Cover design by Monica Bokinskie. Cover art courtesy of Getty Images.

ISSN: 2578-7004 (Print)
ISSN: 2578-7012 (Online)

ISBN: 978-0-8146-6869-6          978-0-8146-6871-9 (e-book)

# Introduction

Just above the doorknob of my office, in a spot I noticed upon entering and leaving each day for thirty years, hung these words from Rabbi Abraham Heschel: *There are no proofs for the existence of God. There are only witnesses.*

Heschel's words were my reminder that the power of God's presence in our lives proclaims not only God's existence but God's very nature. Our lives become an invitation to others to encounter the God we know.

I find myself thinking of the resurrection of Jesus in a similar way. There are no firsthand accounts of the resurrection itself. We do not know if Jesus was lifted up by the hand of his Father or simply awoke on his own, if he unbound himself from the burial cloths or if angels did it for him. We do not know if the resurrection was a quiet event or if it shook the surrounding graves. But what we *do* know is what Jesus' followers witnessed: his bodily presence days after he died and was buried, his familiar voice, his compassion in feeding them as they came in from a long night of fishing, his familiar way of questioning them to aid in their understanding, his authority to send them out to share the Good News.

It is customary to refrain from singing or speaking "Alleluia" throughout the season of Lent. In some parishes the word itself, which literally means "Praise the Lord," is hidden or buried for the period of forty days, then dug up just prior to the Easter Vigil and proclaimed like a burst of joy after a season of self-examination and repentance. The first generation of believers must have initially felt that their reason to praise God had been buried with Jesus, along with their expectations and hopes. Burying and unearthing the "Alleluia" is a symbolic gesture meant to help us, too, long for Good News and new life.

The Easter event and the entire fifty-day season of resurrection are a clarion call to give witness to what we have seen and heard and know to be true: that dying and death never have the last word.

Bring out the "Alleluia"!

Catherine Upchurch

# **Reflections**

## Seeing Is Believing?

**Readings:** Acts 10:34a, 37-43; Col 3:1-4 or 1 Cor 5:6b-8; John 20:1-9 or Luke 24:1-12

**Scripture:**
Then the other disciple also went in, the one who had arrived at the tomb first, and he saw and believed. (John 20:8)

**Reflection:** Have you ever raced to the hospital upon hearing that a family member is giving birth to a child? Or arrived early at a wedding to find a good seat where you know you will be able to see the faces of the bride and groom when they exchange vows? You would not doubt that the marriage or the birth took place if you heard the report from others, but there's something powerful—something both tangibly and intangibly powerful—about being a firsthand witness.

In John's account of the tomb of Jesus, Mary of Magdala is the first to see that something unexpected has happened: the stone covering the entrance to the tomb has been moved. She runs to Simon Peter and the "disciple whom Jesus loved," who both run to the site to see for themselves. All this activity in the early morning hours reveals three things: an empty tomb, burial cloths tossed aside, and the rolled-up cloth that had covered Jesus' head.

We have a saying that "Seeing is believing," but whether that saying is true depends on the seer. A Roman official or a visiting tourist who knows nothing of the man who had been buried there might decide these items are signs of desecration or grave robbery. But the followers of Jesus see something very different. They see proof of life! They have been shaped by their time in the presence of Jesus, by his words and deeds, and by the seeds of hope he has planted in them. Having witnessed what he was all about in life, they have no doubt that he is able to upend death. They see, and they believe. Now they must bear witness.

**Meditation:** In the Acts of the Apostles, Peter says on behalf of the disciples, "We are witnesses of all that he did" (10:39). What Jesus did invites his followers to see who he is and to proclaim it in their actions. Their post-resurrection ministry of healing and teaching in his name introduces Jesus to people who never saw him. How can our lives reflect what Jesus did? Will others know who Jesus is because of us?

**Prayer:** O Lord of the empty tomb, give us eyes to see you even when all seems lost. Make us witnesses to the power of life over death.

## Fearful Yet Overjoyed

**Readings:** Acts 2:14, 22-33; Matt 28:8-15

**Scripture:**
Mary Magdalene and the other Mary went away quickly from the tomb, fearful yet overjoyed. . . . Then Jesus said to them, "Do not be afraid. Go tell my brothers to go to Galilee, and there they will see me." (Matt 28:8, 10)

**Reflection:** The women's response to the angel's message that Jesus has been raised sounds perfectly reasonable to me. Who wouldn't be frightened to see the tomb empty and talk with angels? Who wouldn't also be overjoyed to imagine Jesus is alive, raised from death?

We know from our own experiences that fear and joy can exist within us as companions: becoming parents for the first time, being promoted with added responsibilities, having skills tested on a great adventure, and even facing death after a long and depleting illness. God knows the human heart and gives us the wisdom to hold both realities, fear and joy, until they can become courage.

The risen Jesus seems to know that his followers will need such courage to move forward, and so he asks them to meet him in Galilee. This is the place where they first found the courage to leave their places of comfort and follow a man whose message embodied all they desired. There the disciples (along with women followers, I'm sure) will be reminded of their call to follow Jesus. And there in Galilee, where they first encountered Jesus, they will see the risen Lord for themselves. There, they will be given the courage to proclaim what they know to be true: Jesus has conquered death—not only for himself, but for all of us.

**Meditation:** Where would you return to rediscover the start of your journey with Jesus? The neighborhood or parish of your youth? The location of a meaningful high school retreat? The college where you wrestled with whether to believe at all? The hospital where a serious illness threatened your life or the life of someone you love? There is nothing magical about these locations themselves, but there is something deeply affirming and challenging about meeting Jesus again, as for the first time.

**Prayer:** O Lord of the empty tomb, transform our fears and joys into the courage to proclaim your victory over death.

*April 22: Tuesday within the Octave of Easter*

## Loosening Our Grip

**Readings:** Acts 2:36-41; John 20:11-18

**Scripture:**
Jesus said to her, "Mary! . . . Stop holding on to me." (John 20:16-17)

**Reflection:** Mary Magdalene had been with Jesus throughout his ministry and, according to Luke's Gospel, helped to provide the resources he and his followers needed during his ministry (8:1-3). She was "all in" as we might say today, fully invested. She even stayed with him during his crucifixion and burial. We can well imagine the pain she felt as he died, and the utter confusion that would have enveloped her upon the discovery of the empty tomb.

In one of the most poignant scenes in the New Testament, Mary weeps as she searches for the body of Jesus: "They have taken my Lord, and I don't know where they laid him" (John 20:13). Jesus is her friend, healer, and teacher, but most importantly, he is her Lord. Something that felt like a part of her has been ripped away. When the risen Lord speaks, he first simply says her name, and she recognizes him (as the sheep recognize the voice of the shepherd; John 10:27). Then, in what might feel abrupt or even insensitive, Jesus instructs her to stop holding on to him.

Just as Jesus had earlier released Mary Magdalene from demons and empowered her to follow him, now he is releasing her from what could become an unhealthy clinging to the way things were. The entire ministry of Jesus has demonstrated that nothing ever stays the same upon encountering him: the blind see, the lame walk, the ignorant are instructed. Now, in this raw moment of recognition, Jesus frees Mary to find and be with him in new ways. Her life will testify to his resurrection.

**Meditation:** Deep in our hearts, we yearn to be secure, to be loved and intimately attached to others. Knowing when to let go of one way of loving to allow for a new way of loving is challenging work. Even good things will eventually suffocate if we cling to them too tightly. Where might the risen Jesus be asking you to loosen your grip so that something new can breathe in you?

**Prayer:** O Lord of the empty tomb, never let our longing for the way things were prevent us from moving into the future.

## Nourished by Word and Eucharist

**Readings:** Acts 3:1-10; Luke 24:13-35

**Scripture:**
"Were not our hearts burning within us while he spoke to us on the way and opened the Scriptures to us?" (Luke 24:32)

**Reflection:** When we gather for Mass, whether in our parishes or at the bedside of a family member who is ill, we are nourished at the table of the Word as well as the table of the Eucharist. This moving episode of the disciples traveling to Emmaus beautifully illustrates the connection between the two.

We tend to focus on how the eyes of the disciples are opened as Jesus takes, blesses, breaks, and shares bread with them, a reminder of the same actions Jesus took when he fed the multitude (Luke 9:16) and a foreshadowing of how future generations will forever make present the risen Jesus in the Eucharist. These are vital connections to make. But what prepares the discouraged disciples to recognize Jesus in that moment of sharing bread? His *word*—the way he listened to their longing along the way and addressed it with sound teaching, opening the Scriptures to them.

Whoever these disciples were, and in spite of being told about the empty tomb, they were so deeply distressed—"we were hoping that he would be the one to redeem Israel"— that they could not see Jesus or the kind of redemption he offered. Jesus could simply have said, "It is me, right here with you!" but instead, Jesus chose to listen to their dashed hopes. And in listening, Jesus knew they needed his words and his actions to reveal God's very presence alive with them as they made their way.

Each time we gather to celebrate Mass, we are given that same opportunity: to reflect on our hopes and dreams, identify how Jesus continues to bring the Scriptures to life, and receive the bread and wine of his Body and Blood.

**Meditation:** When have dashed hopes caused you distress or made you wonder, *Where in the world is God?* How has God's presence unfolded in your life during these times? Easter is a season for revelation, for receiving God's ability to feed us in Word and deed, even in the middle of confusion or disbelief.

**Prayer:** O Lord of the empty tomb, just as you listen to us, may we learn to listen to you.

## The Gift of Peace

**Readings:** Acts 3:11-26; Luke 24:35-48

**Scripture:**
[Jesus] stood in their midst and said to them, "Peace be with you." But they were startled and terrified and thought they were seeing a ghost. (Luke 24:36-37)

**Reflection:** I can't help but put myself in the scene of every post-resurrection encounter I hear or read. I have no trouble imagining the confusion, the terror, the fear, and the joy of Jesus' followers. The man who called them to leave it all behind and follow him had been put to death, but he keeps showing up! And he knows what they need: peace.

While a greeting of peace may have been common in the ancient world, Jesus is not just greeting those he meets; he is *gifting* them with a peace that abides. In Hebrew, the word for peace is *shalom,* and it signifies wholeness. We might picture *shalom* as a shattered plate that has been beautifully restored, the seams put together so securely that the plate is even stronger than it was before it was broken.

Think back to the disciples traveling to Emmaus. Broken by their dashed hopes, the risen Lord restored them and made them stronger. His words and actions gifted them with peace. The disciples in today's Gospel have heard the witness of the Emmaus travelers, and just to be sure they understand, the risen Jesus comes into their midst and offers peace.

I chuckle to think how often God's peace is offered when and where the most natural feeling is anything but peace. Perhaps Jesus offers *shalom* as an acknowledgement of the feelings of his followers, knowing it will move them from surface feelings to a deep knowing, the kind of knowing that makes us whole and heals what is broken.

**Meditation:** The lyrics to the hymn "It Is Well with My Soul" were written by Horatio Stafford, a businessman who was financially crippled by the Chicago fire of 1871. Two years after the fire, he sent his wife and four daughters ahead of him to England, where they were to be involved in evangelization efforts. A shipwreck took the life of his daughters. On his crossing to England to join his wife, he penned the words to the now beloved hymn, giving witness to the deep peace that permeated his life even in the midst of immense tragedy. Where might this peace/wholeness/deep-knowing be emerging in your life?

**Prayer:** O Lord of the empty tomb, may your peace become our foundation.

## Revelation Through the Familiar

**Readings:** Acts 4:1-12; John 21:1-14

**Scripture:**
And none of the disciples dared to ask him, "Who are you?" because they realized it was the Lord. (John 21:12)

**Reflection:** Jesus never tires of making himself known. In his post-resurrection encounters he relies on familiar patterns to reveal himself. He calls Mary Magdalene by name so she knows his voice; he teaches with authority and shares bread and wine so the disciples traveling out of Jerusalem will recognize him; he appears to his disciples in familiar places like Galilee or the Upper Room in Jerusalem where they shared their last meal; and in today's Gospel, Jesus meets the fishing disciples on the shore and even cooks a meal for them.

We have an interesting relationship with the familiar. On the one hand, when something is familiar, we can easily overlook it or fail to hear it. This happens, for example, when we hear the stories of Scripture throughout our lives on a three-year loop in the liturgy. A passage can become so familiar that we essentially fail to listen to it. It happens too when we're busy looking for extraordinary occurrences instead of finding the extraordinary in the ordinary. The English writer G. K. Chesterton says we must "learn to look at things familiar until they look unfamiliar again."

On the other hand, the familiar can attract us, put us at ease, and coax us into feeling receptive. It is this side of familiarity that Jesus draws upon when meeting his closest followers. The familiar way he spoke and taught and came to the shore becomes the avenue to insight and joy for the disciples. In their witness to his resurrection, the disciples will imitate his use of the familiar to introduce others to the extraordinary.

**Meditation:** Consider how Jesus makes himself known to you and to others you know well. What is the usual path of revelation? Is it through something entirely out of the ordinary or through what is simple and familiar? Does your experience teach you something about how you might help others discover Jesus in their midst?

**Prayer:** O Lord of the empty tomb, visit us in the familiar to lead us to the extraordinary.

## Compelled to Share Good News

**Readings:** Acts 4:13-21; Mark 16:9-15

**Scripture:**
"It is impossible for us not to speak about what we have seen and heard." (Acts 4:20)

**Reflection:** "You won't believe this." "Buckle up, have I got a story to tell you!" "This is going to blow your mind." There are dozens of ways we prepare people to hear news that is baffling, news that we ourselves might have trouble comprehending, news that could well be transformative. In today's scene from the Acts of the Apostles, Peter and John have been telling the story of Jesus in their preaching and in their acts of healing. The Jewish high court, known as the Sanhedrin, cannot deny what they are seeing and hearing, but they want it stopped. It's upsetting the normal course of affairs and stirring up the people.

We cannot know precisely why the Sanhedrin takes the step of trying to silence Peter and John. It could be out of jealousy over Jesus' continuing popularity even after the crucifixion. It could be that they fear the people will cause an uproar that gets the attention of the Roman occupiers, who will then make life harder for the Jews. It could even be a result of their own confusion about how to respond to what they see happening before their very eyes. In any case, the apostles know that they cannot help but proclaim what they have witnessed. And they probably also know that they could very well get themselves in hot water.

Today's reading from Mark's Gospel sets the stage for the unadorned truth of Jesus to be preached throughout the world. Having not believed Mary Magdalene nor the disciples whom Jesus accompanied "on their way to the country," the eleven remaining disciples are rebuked by Jesus for their unbelief yet are trusted to be sent out to proclaim the Gospel to every creature.

**Meditation:** What do we want our families to know about Jesus? How do we share with our neighbors what we have experienced and believe? And more importantly, how does our life testify that even the unbelievable—rising from the dead, God's immeasurable mercy and love—can be believed and trusted?

**Prayer:** O Lord of the empty tomb, may we find it impossible not to speak of your action in our lives.

*April 27: Second Sunday of Easter*
*(Sunday of Divine Mercy)*

## Enduring Love and Mercy

**Readings:** Acts 5:12-16; Rev 1:9-11a, 12-13, 17-19; John 20:19-31

**Scripture:**
Give thanks to the Lord for he is good,
   his love is everlasting. (Ps 118:1)

**Reflection:** Alternate translations for our psalm refrain today include "his mercy endures forever" and "his loving-kindness is without end." These variations tell us something about the rich meaning of the original Hebrew term, *hesed*.

First and foremost, *hesed* is not a feeling but a way of being. It is the very nature of God, who is the fullness of loving mercy. Every action of God on behalf of those in need (and aren't we all in need?) is an act of unmerited mercy. Not having earned this loving-kindness, we can only receive it in gratitude.

Second, God's *hesed* is not a rare or even an occasional kindness. It is everlasting and enduring. It is tenacious even in the face of ingratitude, wrapping us like a garment that is needed in the event of storms or enjoyed in the light of calm sunrises. God's mercy holds us close even when we are unaware of it.

In a great act of mercy, Jesus willingly dies and rises to show us that death never has the final word, not only for him but for all of us. Death in the form of self-doubt receives the mercy of knowing one's worth. Death as disobedience to God's law receives the mercy of forgiveness and firm resolve. Death in terms of violence receives the mercy of compassion and self-control.

The Easter season invites us to meditate on our God who not only *gives* love and mercy but *is* love and mercy.

**Meditation:** Many of us grew up with images of God that failed to account for God's loving-kindness. Rather than appreciating the liberation of slaves in Egypt and the giving of the Ten Commandments as an act of God's mercy, for example, we may have focused on a God who demands obedience. Instead of understanding God's desire to form a people as characterized by mercy and justice, we may have thought of God as a friend to some and an enemy to others. The Easter season invites us to see God through the lenses of *hesed* and new life.

**Prayer:** O God whose mercy endures, use our efforts to reach those who are in most need of faith in your goodness.

## Spiritual Rebirth

**Readings:** Acts 4:23-31; John 3:1-8

**Scripture:**
"How can a man once grown old be born again?" (John 3:4)

**Reflection:** I have lived in parts of the country where it is not unusual to be asked, "Are you born again?" My typical response—"Every day, without fail!"—either firmly closes the door to a conversation or opens it wide; there is usually no in-between. I love these opportunities to talk together about what "born again" means in our varied religious traditions, and what it means in our individual lives.

All of us have some experience with birth, either the stories from our own births, being present during a birth, or giving birth to a child oneself. Our birth is evident by our mere presence. But a re-birth? Being born *again*?

Nicodemus approaches Jesus and begins with an affirmation: "No one can do these signs that you are doing unless God is with him." Jesus wastes no time in turning this encounter into an opportunity to draw Nicodemus into a deeper understanding of the kingdom of God. Just as we are born in the flesh at a particular point in time, we must also be born afresh in water and the spirit. It's not enough to be baptized in water if we do not also experience a spiritual baptism, a conversion of how we live as a result of being baptized.

We don't typically receive this spiritual conversion all in one moment, though some of us may be able to identify dramatic moments of change. Dramatic or not, conversion is an ongoing process that evolves and deepens over the course of our lives through prayer, persistent desire to draw nearer to God, seeking wisdom from our life experiences, and participating in building the kingdom through acts of mercy and justice.

**Meditation:** Sometimes we limit our experience of God to well-worn expectations ("God will always . . ." or "God would never . . ."). Jesus both fulfills typical expectations and shatters them. His very presence is proof that God works in unexpected and even shocking ways. How does Jesus' creative use of normal images open up new possibilities?

**Prayer:** O God whose mercy endures, speak with us in ways that expand our experiences and expectations.

April 29: Saint Catherine of Siena

# The Power of the Resurrection

**Readings:** Acts 4:32-37; John 3:7b-15

**Scripture:**
With great power the Apostles bore witness to the resurrection of the Lord Jesus. . . . There was no needy person among them. (Acts 4:33-34)

**Reflection:** I have read this passage from the Acts of the Apostles many times, but as I prepared to write this reflection, I noticed something new.

I was aware that the apostles courageously bore witness to Jesus and to his resurrection. No one can deny that rising from the dead is a miraculous sign of God's power. It is cause for amazement, a reason for celebration, and a source of inner conviction. For those who followed Jesus, his resurrection was proof of his identity, settling any doubts or misgivings they may have had, and giving them the perfect opening to attract additional followers as they spread this remarkable news. The testimony of the apostles was not possible without the power of God working within and among them.

Today's passage from Acts is saturated with descriptions of the ideal community of believers: united in heart and mind, sharing possessions, and even selling off property to support those in need in the community. Right in the middle

**24**   *Saint Catherine of Siena*

of this picture, we are told that the apostles bore witness to the resurrection. This is where a new insight emerged in my reflections: there is an inescapable connection between bearing witness to the resurrection and serving the needs of the community.

If the resurrection only serves to "wow" us or to give us hope of our own resurrection, we have missed something essential. If we are to be resurrection people, we must be transformed. Our actions must demonstrate that we serve the living God, the God who is not afraid to reach into the human condition and lift us all out of our limitations.

**Meditation:** If you could paint a picture of your parish, alive with the power of the resurrection, what would it look like? Would there be changes in your community life? In your liturgical life? In your service to the broader neighborhood?

**Prayer:** O God whose mercy endures, may new life stream from acts of service given and received.

## God Wills Salvation

**Readings:** Acts 5:17-26; John 3:16-21

**Scripture:**
For God did not send his Son into the world to condemn the world, but that the world might be saved through him. (John 3:17)

**Reflection:** I once heard a preacher say he was tired of the "soft Jesus" that so many preach and that he believed Jesus was anything but "soft." I agree with that preacher, but I think he and I understand his sentiment in different ways. His preaching revealed that he believed God's judgment and condemnation are missing in the way some people relate to Jesus, and that Jesus' promises only apply to those who repent in fear and trembling. His Jesus is not "soft on crime" or "soft on sin."

But I wonder what kind of witness we give to the risen Lord when, instead, we believe deeply that God's intent is to save the world, not condemn it. I do not think that softens our depiction of Jesus; I believe it strengthens it. Jesus embodies what it means to find strength in justice and love and mercy, the qualities of God and God's covenant with us. A tyrant is capable of barking orders and pronouncing condemnation, but a tyrant is not capable of deep instruction or inviting people to self-examination as Jesus did.

God, who is revealed to us throughout Scripture, particularly in the person of Jesus, is anything but soft. Jesus' standards are high, but they are not imposed on us. His judgment is always given with an eye to conversion rather than condemnation. Obedience out of fear will not result in the freedom needed to respond to God in love. And it is only when we respond freely that we are drawn out of darkness into the light that is Jesus.

**Meditation:** Today's reading from John's Gospel begins with the words "God so loved the world." The measure of God's love is sending Jesus, not to pluck us out of the human condition, or to rescue us from the evil around us, or even to rescue us from ourselves. The mission of Jesus is to save us in the very circumstances of chaos and evil that are part of the human condition.

**Prayer:** O God whose mercy endures, draw us to you with cords of love and fill us with strength to live the full truth of who you are.

*May 1: Thursday of the Second Week of Easter*
*(Saint Joseph the Worker)*

## Foreshadowing the Resurrection

**Readings:** Acts 5:27-33; John 3:31-36; or Gen 1:26–2:3 or Col 3:14-15, 17, 23-24; Matt 13:54-58

**Scripture:**
Jesus came to his native place and taught the people in their synagogue. They were astonished and said, "Where did this man get such wisdom and mighty deeds? Is he not the carpenter's son?" (Matt 13:54-55)

**Reflection:** It is helpful to remember that the Gospels were not written as eyewitness, on-the-spot reports. Instead, they are the result of decades of reflection and evangelization after the death and resurrection of Jesus. Jesus rose from the dead, commissioned his followers to spread the Good News, and then ascended to heaven before sending the Spirit. When the Gospel stories were eventually written, naturally they were told through the lens of the resurrection of Jesus. How could it be otherwise?

On this feast of Saint Joseph the Worker, we have the opportunity to ponder how the resurrection of Jesus "creeps" its way backward into an earlier scene of Jesus teaching in his hometown. Where might we find bits of evidence that point us to the empty tomb? What are the breadcrumbs that lead the way to this triumph of life over death?

First, the people in Jesus' hometown are astounded that one of their own is able to perform mighty deeds, just as his apostles are later astounded by the ultimate mighty deed of rising from the dead. Second, some in his hometown take offense at Jesus, just as some in Jerusalem, particularly religious leaders, take offense at his resurrection. In both locations, Jesus encounters a lack of faith. And in both situations, none of these barriers halt his mission as God's Son, nor distance him from his identity as the son of Joseph, the carpenter.

**Meditation:** As the apostles and others began their work spreading the Good News, we can imagine the first stories they must have told. We might think they would begin with the birth of Jesus, but this is unlikely. The most astounding proof of Jesus' identity is his resurrection. Once the evangelists told this earth-shifting story, the rest of the pieces would follow: his mission, his roots, his birth. Where do you begin telling the story of Jesus in your life when sharing with others?

**Prayer:** O God whose mercy endures, may the resurrection of Jesus transform our vision and allow us to see the events of our lives through the lens of new life.

## Pausing for Discernment

**Readings:** Acts 5:34-42; John 6:1-15

**Scripture:**
"[I]f this endeavor or this activity is of human origin, it will destroy itself. But if it comes from God, you will not be able to destroy them; you may even find yourselves fighting against God." (Acts 5:38-39)

**Reflection:** Pharisees are often given a pretty bad rap in the Gospels. Apparently, there were a good number of them who were extremely strident about obedience to religious law, and some were accused of hypocrisy as well. But we need to be careful not to paint all Pharisees with one wide brush. The Pharisees were lay leaders (teachers and scribes) who believed that clear adherence to the law of Moses and the oral traditions surrounding it would maintain Jewish identity in an increasingly pluralistic society—not a bad idea at its core.

Today's reading from Acts finds us privy to a discussion taking place within the Sanhedrin, the supreme religious court in Jerusalem, determining what to do with the followers of Jesus who continue to preach and heal in his name. Among the group is Gamaliel, identified as a Pharisee. Gamaliel disproves the popular idea that all Pharisees were stridently opposed to Jesus and his followers. His advice to refrain from punishing the apostles of Jesus, allowing God and time to sort it out, was wisely accepted.

A great piece of advice I received years ago, and one that has gained popularity on social media, is to pause in the heat of a moment. It is not possible to wisely discern solutions to problems or to formulate sound responses to hurt or injustice when our feelings are heated.

For people of faith, that "sacred pause" becomes not just a time for cooling down but a time to pray and seek wisdom.

**Meditation:** Just because I have been given sound advice does not mean I always adhere to it! But I can cultivate habits that will assist me. In order to pause in the heat of a moment of confusion or anger, for example, I can train myself to pause in other moments as well. In this way, pausing is not an unusual occurrence but becomes part of my spiritual muscle memory. What habits might we create to help us pause, to give ourselves space and time to seek wisdom when times are difficult?

**Prayer:** O God whose mercy endures, guide us to your wisdom, especially in moments that are filled with emotion.

## No More Wishful Thinking

**Readings:** 1 Cor 15:1-8; John 14:6-14

**Scripture:**
"Amen, amen, I say to you, whoever believes in me will do the works that I do, and will do greater ones than these, because I am going to the Father." (John 14:12)

**Reflection:** I've heard people say that they wish they had lived in Israel at the time of Jesus' ministry so they could have witnessed for themselves how he taught and healed. Then, they say, *then* they could believe in him. Of course, we might remind them that even those who were with Jesus daily didn't always "get it." In fact, we might be at an advantage because we have been given the gift of the Spirit and two thousand years of living witnesses.

On some level, today's Gospel addresses that sense of wishful thinking. Jesus and his apostles are gathered in Jerusalem, sharing their final meal together, and there is undoubtedly a sense of foreboding in the air. Judas has been identified as the one who will betray Jesus, and Peter as the one who will deny knowing him. Jesus uses this time to settle their troubled hearts with words of encouragement about the essential role they will play in continuing the works of Jesus.

In fact, Jesus tells his followers something that would sound scandalous if it were not attributed to Jesus himself:

they will do even greater works than he did! How can this be? Jesus will share with them (and with us) the unity he has with the Father, and he will send the Spirit as a sign of his continuing presence with them. The Acts of the Apostles is filled with instances of the work of the living Jesus continuing in and through the earliest generation of believers. Christian history gives us further testimony that God is still doing wonderful things among us.

**Meditation:** When has wishful thinking prevented you from living in the present moment and recognizing its potential? "If I had only seen . . ." or "If God had only . . . ." Ironically, by wishing things had been different in the past, we can fail to make a difference in the now. Let's invite God's gift of the Spirit to help us give witness to where God is at work today.

**Prayer:** O God whose mercy endures, may we find you at work in our words and deeds so that we truly become the living Body of Christ.

## **Always a Follower**

**Readings:** Acts 5:27-32, 40b-41; Rev 5:11-14; John 21:1-19 or 21:1-14

**Scripture:**
"Simon, son of John, do you love me? . . . Feed my sheep. . . . Follow me." (John 21:17, 19)

**Reflection:** I can still picture my grade school class forming a neat and tidy line to follow our teachers in and out of the school building or church. As we got older, we were sometimes given the opportunity to lead that line of students; we felt so accomplished when it was our turn! Who didn't want to graduate to head of the line? And yet, the final verse of today's Gospel got me thinking about the value of being a good follower.

The dialogue between Jesus and Peter, including Jesus' instruction to Peter to feed his sheep, is part of our understanding of the primacy of Peter and his role as a leader among leaders in the early church. Take note, though, that even the first universal pastor is instructed to be a follower of Jesus. Peter's role is not about power but about always following Jesus.

But what does that following look like? Peter and the other leaders of the church follow Jesus through death and resurrection to be sure. They will also follow Jesus when they ponder and obey his teachings, when they provide food for the hungry to eat and living water for the thirsty, when they speak the truth in difficult situations, and when they humbly serve the least among us. Such following does not signify weakness but is actually the key to leadership.

Whether we are called to lead as a bishop or pastor, or as a parent or teacher, we never stop being a disciple, a follower of Jesus.

**Meditation:** A disciple is one who follows, and a disciple of Jesus is one who follows Jesus. Unlike in a school setting where we find definite beginnings and endings, and where success is noted by reaching measurable goals, a disciple of Christ is always learning, responding, and learning some more. The measurable goal of a disciple is how we are continuously being transformed into the image of Christ who leads us. What are some of the ways that being a disciple tempers our egos and directs us toward humble service?

**Prayer:** O God, draw us near, and give us hearts for discipleship rather than power.

## Not Wowed but Roused

**Readings:** Acts 6:8-15; John 6:22-29

**Scripture:**
"Amen, amen, I say to you, you are looking for me not because you saw signs but because you ate the loaves and were filled." (John 6:26)

**Reflection:** Human beings have a deep desire to find meaning in life. We want to know that our lives matter and our daily routines are not meaningless. We may be tempted to look for meaning in fleeting things—the number of followers or "likes" we have on social media, the satisfaction of being in the "in crowd," or the status that comes with climbing the corporate ladder. While none of these things are harmful in themselves, they can be an indication that we are seeking something more—something that is truly fulfilling.

Today's Gospel comes from the Bread of Life discourse in the Gospel of John. The words and actions of Jesus highlight what is truly nourishing for our lives. Those who followed Jesus across the Sea of Galilee from Tiberias to Capernaum could not help but be attracted to him. He had taken a few simple loaves and fish and fed a massive crowd. He was a wonder-worker, and they were anxious to see more. But Jesus wants to ensure that the people are not simply "wowed" but "roused," that they will look beyond the multiplication of food to the one who will truly feed them, and that every person will know who can give them the "food that endures for eternal life."

**Meditation:** Much of what we seek or accumulate is not lasting: a temporary high from a wonderful vacation, social media connections instead of enduring friendships, a rare piece of jewelry that we tuck away in a safe deposit box. This kind of seeking can creep into our spiritual lives easily enough. Perhaps our worship is not as lively with a new liturgist or pastor, and we're tempted to seek a different experience elsewhere. Or perhaps a dry spell in prayer has us wondering if it really matters to be faithful to the practice. Jesus invites us to dig deep and find what is lasting and true beyond tangible but often temporary objects or experiences.

**Prayer:** O God, draw us near, enliven us with gifts that endure and insight that is true.

## Echoing Jesus

**Readings:** Acts 7:51–8:1a; John 6:30-35

**Scripture:**
As they were stoning Stephen, he called out, "Lord Jesus, receive my spirit." Then he fell to his knees and cried out in a loud voice, "Lord, do not hold this sin against them." (Acts 7:59-60)

**Reflection:** The Bible is filled with echoes—sounds, phrases, and scenes that bounce forward and backward in time so we take notice. Today's scene of the stoning of Stephen found in the Acts of the Apostles echoes the lament and trust found in Psalm 31. The psalmist, in distress and spirits flagging, cries out: "Into your hands I commend my spirit; / you will redeem me, O Lord, O faithful God" (31:6). Centuries later, Jesus cries out to God from the cross another echo of this verse: "Father, into your hands I commend my spirit" (Luke 23:46). The psalmist, Jesus, and Stephen all call attention to the necessity of surrendering ourselves to God, a disposition that is only possible in the context of trusting God.

Another echo is heard in Stephen's words begging God to "not hold this sin" against those who are stoning him to death. Just as Jesus had asked his Father to forgive his executioners (and in truth those who pronounced a death sentence upon him), Stephen's words show a generosity of spirit that is truly Christ-like (Luke 23:34).

At the start of this week, we pondered why leaders must still be disciples, ones who follow. The author of Acts recounts the story of Stephen as a clear example of what it looks like to follow Jesus, to echo him, even in the manner of surrender and forgiveness at the moment of death. Through the centuries, all kinds of saints, canonized as well as those unknown to us, have borne witness to this power of discipleship.

**Meditation:** Have you ever met someone and almost immediately recognized familiar facial features or mannerisms? It may take a moment or two, but eventually you may be able to identify the person's family just by watching and listening. Imagine what it would be like for people to meet us, pause for a few moments, and recognize us as members of Jesus' family.

**Prayer:** O God, draw us near, so that we become more able and willing to echo the sounds and works of Jesus in our world.

## Nothing Is Lost

**Readings:** Acts 8:1b-8; John 6:35-40

**Scripture:**
"And this is the will of the one who sent me, that I should not lose anything of what he gave me." (John 6:39)

**Reflection:** Readers of the Gospel of John will notice that there are stark contrasts to be found there: darkness and light, the new covenant and the old, the kingdom of God and the kingdom of this world. Jesus draws clear lines for his followers, urging them to choose whether they're in or out. Sometimes this has led to an image of Jesus as harsh and judgmental, holding out promises of eternal life only for those who choose rightly. But perhaps we are the ones emphasizing who is in and who is out.

The Gospel of John highlights the unity of Jesus and the Father, making it clear that Jesus' authority comes from the Father and that his actions reflect the will of the Father. In today's Gospel, the will of the Father is that Jesus not lose anything of what he has been given. And what has he been given? The entire world! For what purpose? The salvation of the world: "For God did not send his Son into the world to condemn the world, but that the world might be saved through him" (John 3:17).

If God wills salvation for the world, then we share in this task by demonstrating how much God loves the world and all who populate it. In this way, like Jesus, we hold out hope of eternal life not just for those who share our profession of faith in Jesus, but for all who are within reach of his voice.

**Meditation:** Earlier in the Gospel of John, when Jesus fed the multitude with a small amount of food, he instructed the disciples, "Gather the fragments left over, so that nothing will be wasted" (6:12). They filled a dozen baskets as yet another sign that in God's kingdom, nothing is lost. Our witness about who God is may fall on deaf ears or hardened hearts—and it may well be that our hearts could use some softening, too—but God uses our efforts as grace in ways we may not see.

**Prayer:** O God, draw us near, keep us close to your Son who willingly gathers the leftovers and reaches out to us when we are lost.

*May 8: Thursday of the Third Week of Easter*

## Teaching that Leads to Christ

**Readings:** Acts 8:26-40; John 6:44-51

**Scripture:**
Philip ran up and heard [the eunuch] reading Isaiah the prophet and said, "Do you understand what you are reading?" He replied, "How can I, unless someone instructs me?" (Acts 8:30-31)

**Reflection:** I often find myself thinking of my teachers from grade school through graduate school, and I've noticed that my favorites are those who possessed certain qualities: an ability to recognize teachable moments, a deep sense of joy (though I know classroom teaching is far from easy), knowledge and passion for their subject matter, and love for the students right in front of them.

The apostle Philip strikes me as this kind of teacher. He recognizes a "teachable moment" as the eunuch's chariot passes by and he hears the man reading aloud (quite a normal practice in the ancient world among the literate). Philip's joy and knowledge in instructing the Ethiopian is obvious; he not only explains the Isaiah passage but uses it as the starting point to proclaim Jesus as he knew him and as the fulfillment of Scripture. And best of all, Philip loves this hungry inquirer so much that he doesn't hesitate to baptize him, though baptism of Gentiles was not yet an approved or standard practice among the Jews who followed Jesus.

Philip knew the Lord Jesus in a personal way and surely experienced Jesus as the Bread of Life that we hear about in today's Gospel reading. In his teaching, as in the teaching of Jesus, Philip relies on God to use his words, his instincts and knowledge, and his love and joy to instruct the traveler. Instruction, though, is never an end in itself. It opens hearts and minds, and it offers a new lens through which to see the world. Instruction in the Christian context always has the potential to evangelize.

**Meditation:** We draw from a great storehouse of teachings when we instruct children and adults so their understanding of faith grows and their ability to apply these teachings is expanded. However, our catechesis (instruction) will mean nothing if it is not accompanied by proclaiming how Jesus is alive and active in our lives, allowing the opportunity to encounter Christ (the heart of evangelization).

**Prayer:** O God, draw us near, and help us to value Jesus' teachings as we also value building a relationship with him.

## The Power of Humility

**Readings:** Acts 9:1-20; John 6:52-59

**Scripture:**
Ananias went and entered the house; laying hands on him, he said, "Saul, my brother, the Lord has sent me." (Acts 9:17)

**Reflection:** Ananias strikes me as a man of humility and bravery. Saul's reputation had preceded him: he was intent on arresting and imprisoning the newly emerging group of Jews who believed Jesus was the Christ, and he had the authority of the Sanhedrin to back him up. Understandably, Ananias, a Christ-follower, is troubled by the reports and is hesitant to go as God commands and offer Saul healing from his recent blindness. His reluctance reminds me of Israel's prophets, all of whom protested when God commissioned them to speak in his name to the people of Israel and Judah, especially to resistant religious and political leaders.

We are given little insight into the inner dialogue going on in Ananias's mind and heart, but we can well imagine that he had to be humble enough to be obedient to God. Authentically humble people do not think poorly of themselves but recognize that they share much in common with every other person, and that sometimes they need to admit that they cannot see the bigger picture. God sees the bigger picture in regard to both Saul *and* Ananias. The opportunity for Ananias to do the hard thing will be transforming for both of them.

Ananias greets Saul, the man he knows to be a persecutor, as a brother. This acknowledgment of their shared humanity probably opened a door that would otherwise have remained locked. It takes great courage to be obedient to God and to believe that enemies can become friends and violence can become peace. Without these singular efforts, like Ananias going to Saul, the larger efforts of transforming the world would not happen.

**Meditation:** St. Thomas Aquinas says humility is "seeing ourselves as God sees us: knowing every good we have comes from God as pure gift." In a culture that values the person who is "self-made," humility can be seen as a weakness rather than the strength of prioritizing a deep sense of harmony with others and with creation.

**Prayer:** O God, draw us near, and share with us the gift of humility so we can be contributors in our world and not bystanders.

## Where Is Our Allegiance?

**Readings:** Acts 9:31-42; John 6:60-69

**Scripture:**
Jesus then said to the Twelve, "Do you also want to leave?"
Simon Peter answered him, "Master, to whom shall we go?
You have the words of eternal life." (John 6:67-68)

**Reflection:** Today's Gospel scene is set in Capernaum, the
area that was pretty much home base for Jesus' ministry in
Galilee. People here had listened to the heart of Jesus' teaching and witnessed him offering healing (Jairus's daughter,
the woman who touched his cloak, the paralyzed man
brought by his friends, and Peter's mother-in-law, to name
a few). Today's scene occurs just after Jesus has told his followers that he is the Bread of Life who gives his flesh for the
life of the world. While that may sound like good news all
these centuries later, there were many listeners who found
it hard to accept and, in their discouragement, began to leave
Jesus.

In this critical moment, Jesus asks those closest to him if
they too will leave. It had to be tempting for his disciples to
at least consider it, given the controversy that Jesus stirred
up, the resistance he met, and the difficulty they may have
foreseen in living this new way of life. But they stay: "Master,
to whom shall we go?"

This is a question that every follower of Jesus has to ponder at one time or another. Something or someone will always demand our allegiance. Our choice about who or what to follow, who or what to love, will determine everything.

I believe the disciples stayed because they loved Jesus. Their commitment grew in response to allowing themselves to be loved, to be entrusted with a share in building the kingdom of God that Jesus envisioned and shared. The value of staying with Jesus far outweighed the impulse to leave.

What more will they learn from him? How will he give them cause for hope?

**Meditation:** Not everyone who turns to Jesus receives the healing they desire or the solution to a problem they voice. When it seems unfair or too demanding to wrestle with these realities, we may be tempted to turn away. But God asks us to look more deeply, to imagine the world without the vision of the kingdom of God or without a cause for hope.

**Prayer:** O God, draw us near, and give us the desire to stay with you even when the way seems difficult.

## Knowing the Shepherd

**Readings:** Acts 13:14, 43-52; Rev 7:9, 14b-17; John 10:27-30

**Scripture:**
"My sheep hear my voice; I know them, and they follow me." (John 10:27)

**Reflection:** Sheep and shepherds are quite plentiful throughout the Bible, and they were quite plentiful throughout the ancient Middle East. The shepherd image is used to describe God in the Psalms and the books of the prophets. It is little wonder that Jesus describes his role and identity using this image; most everyone would have connected to it in some practical or religious way.

When Jesus spent time in the desert, or in a quiet place where he went for prayer, I picture him observing shepherds with their flocks, scattered across hillsides, searching for sustenance and protection from the extreme elements. He would have seen small groups of shepherds draw all of their sheep together at night to remain safe and secure until the morning light. Then, once again, the sheep would be separated, each flock going along with its own shepherd. Perhaps this is where Jesus pondered how the sheep knew which shepherd to follow.

Both the sheep and the shepherd had to learn to recognize one another. Was it that kind of mutual recognition that Jesus hoped he and his followers would have? In the midst of all the noise of society, Jesus is inviting us to listen for his voice, to learn to distinguish his message from others.

We will follow Jesus, like sheep follow their shepherd, as we learn that his voice is true and loving, and his words contain the message of life.

**Meditation:** It strikes me that Jesus is patient in guiding us to recognize and listen to his voice. But what about us? How do we cut through the noise around us so we are able to hear him? Will that require more than just desire? What spiritual disciplines might help us learn to listen for the voice of Jesus? How might immersion in Scripture and exposure to sound teaching help us become more discerning? Would it serve us well to consider how we spend our time and with whom?

**Prayer:** Good and gracious Shepherd, call to us until we know your voice, and create in us the desire to follow you.

## The Way to Salvation

**Readings:** Acts 11:1-18; John 10:1-10

**Scripture:**
"I am the gate. Whoever enters through me will be saved, and will come in and go out and find pasture. A thief comes only to steal and slaughter and destroy; I came so that they might have life and have it more abundantly." (John 10:9-10)

**Reflection:** What does it mean to be saved? Jesus says if we "enter the pasture" through him, the gate, we will be saved. But what does that mean? Saved from what and for what? The simplest answer to these questions is that we are saved from sin, and that the purpose of our salvation is to serve God and others as we hold onto the promise of eternal life.

At the risk of sounding like a broken record, we might ask again what all of this really means. Today's Gospel reading from John offers us a slightly different way to look at salvation. If Jesus comes to give abundant life, could that be a definition of salvation? And if Jesus provides the gateway to abundant life, perhaps the abundance he speaks of is what he himself embodies—mercy, joy, justice, peace, truth, hope, and compassion. By knowing what we are saved *for*, we can better understand what we are saved *from*. Jesus saves us from whatever prevents us from experiencing the abundance he brings. Sinful attitudes and behaviors, addictions, and a false sense of security are but a few of the things that Jesus saves us from, if we let him.

While some people might confuse this promise of abundant life with prosperity, nothing could be further from the truth. God's abundance is available for all people—rich and poor, educated and uneducated, healthy and unhealthy. As we hear in today's reading from Acts, God gives the "same gift" (11:17)—this abundant life—to both Jews and Gentiles, to all who are willing to receive it.

**Meditation:** The God who fashioned us and continues to shape us knows that each one of us is worthy of living abundantly. We're the ones who sometimes don't recognize or accept this gracious gift of God. Have we grown used to living with a sense of spiritual scarcity, as if God doesn't have enough grace to go around? Or enough patience to wait for us?

**Prayer:** Good and gracious Shepherd, open wide our hearts so your life of abundance can become our deepest desire and we can give witness to your generous offer of salvation.

## Grace That Can Be Seen

**Readings:** Acts 11:19-26; John 10:22-30

**Scripture:**
When [Barnabas] arrived and saw the grace of God, he rejoiced and encouraged them all to remain faithful to the Lord in firmness of heart. (Acts 11:23)

**Reflection:** When I was young, I learned that grace was like filling a glass with water: as we "drank" the grace, we could always ask for more. This image made grace seem like something rather limited, something that could be portioned out. Now, long past my childhood years, I think of grace more like an ocean: vast and constant in its rhythms. As the ocean never ceases to seek the shore, grace never ceases to seek us. And unlike that clear glass of water, the ocean is filled with all kinds of living activity. Perhaps grace is the same.

Barnabas sees the grace of God when he arrives at Antioch. I've seen the grace of God, and I'll wager you have too. We tend to think of grace as something intangible, but in reality, grace is teeming with life and activity. It is manifested in serving others in need, comforting those who are mourning a loss, becoming a source of healing when bodies and hearts are broken, visiting the imprisoned, and welcoming the stranger in our midst. Our Gospel today reminds us that even the works of Jesus are manifestations of God's grace: "The works I do in my Father's name testify to me."

Grace is evidence of God's life in us, teeming with activity. Transformed by this grace, we give witness to who God is and how God acts in the world. The vastness of God's grace allows us, even compels us, to contribute to transforming the world one loving action at a time.

**Meditation:** Awareness of God alive and active in the world is a pillar of the spiritual life. Awareness that our values, words, and actions reveal who God is to us can become grace for someone else, someone who feels lost or confused. When have another person's actions revealed the grace of God to you? How might your interactions with others become part of that graceful tide of God's love?

**Prayer:** Good and gracious Shepherd, let us tap into the ocean of grace that is forever coming ashore, and invite us to come into deeper waters with you.

## No Greater Love

**Readings:** Acts 1:15-17, 20-26; John 15:9-17

**Scripture:**
"No one has greater lover than this, to lay down one's life for one's friends." (John 15:13)

**Reflection:** There is nothing quite like the security of knowing we can confide in a friend. In the comfort of true friendship, we can reveal everything about ourselves, and over time that kind of continuing conversation creates a deep bond of trust. We can expect to give and receive advice, truth, and kindness.

Jesus offers this kind of friendship to us. He's even willing to tell us everything he has heard from his Father rather than keeping it to himself. He's teaching us that the nature of love is to give it all away.

As we well know, just as love has much to give, it also comes at a price. For Jesus, the price is his very life. Over the centuries, beginning with most of the apostles, others have given their lives in love as well—Saint Oscar Romero, the storied martyrs of Uganda, Maximilian Kolbe, Ita Ford, Maura Clarke, Dorothy Kazel, Jean Donovan, and Dorothy Stang, to name just a few. We would be right in saying that sometimes friendship with Jesus can be quite costly.

The good news of this Easter season is that even at so great a price as martyrdom, death does not have the final word. Love does. We remember the martyrs not primarily for the ways they died, but for the kind of love that put them in places of great need and gave them courage to face great danger—the kind of love that can't help but share the Good News of their friend Jesus.

**Meditation:** It might seem odd to focus on the cost of discipleship during this Easter season. But what better time is there to be reminded of the power of sacrificial love? Tertullian, a second-century writer from Carthage, said that "the blood of the martyrs is the seed of the church." Nonbelievers sought out Christians to find out what made Jesus worth dying for. What reason would you give?

**Prayer:** Good and gracious Shepherd, befriend us in good times and in bad, and stay with us through danger as we bear witness to your love.

## God Is Good

**Readings:** Acts 13:13-25; John 13:16-20

**Scripture:**
For ever I will sing the goodness of the Lord. (Ps 89:2)

**Reflection:** During the Easter season, we are treated to stories of the exploits and travels of the apostles after the resurrection and ascension of Jesus, as told in the Acts of the Apostles. These earliest evangelists, empowered by the command of Jesus to go out into all the world preaching the Good News, did just that. In a matter of about thirty years, Christianity caught hold across the expanse of the Roman Empire. And this happened without planes, trains, and automobiles, even without the conveniences of instant communication or plentiful hotels in which to stay. Needless to say, if the apostles felt daunted by their commission from Jesus, the Spirit must have given them the energy and stamina to do the work.

The first generation of Christian evangelists proclaimed the goodness of the Lord. It's safe to say that Christians took up where their ancestors in faith left off. Israel knew the goodness of God firsthand as they were liberated from slavery, received God's covenant, settled in the Promised Land, and established a monarchy. They knew God's goodness even in exile. Many Jews recognized in Jesus the fulfillment of God's promises, and many who were not Jewish came to believe that God's covenant with Israel had been extended to include them. God indeed is good.

Every ongoing proclamation of God's goodness is also a reminder to us to be ambassadors of that goodness. Our words and deeds reflect to others not only who we are but who God is for us.

**Meditation:** Keeping a gratitude journal has become popular in recent years, partly because it's a healthy psychological practice resulting in better sleep habits and a calmer disposition. Gratitude is an essential part of our spiritual lives as well. Maybe we could adapt this practice a little, keeping a journal not of our gratitude but of God's goodness. This can sharpen our ability to see God at work not just in our own lives but in the entire world.

**Prayer:** Good and gracious Shepherd, renew within us the fervor of those first evangelists as we too proclaim your goodness.

## The Power of Dwelling

**Readings:** Acts 13:26-33; John 14:1-6

**Scripture:**
"And if I go and prepare a place for you, I will come back again and take you to myself, so that where I am you also may be." (John 14:3)

**Reflection:** One of the most startling and almost incomprehensible things about Jesus is that he became one of us at a particular point in time. God chose to do more than figuratively walk with us; God chose to be fully united with us—born of a woman, raised in a typical Jewish household, and educated in the faith tradition of Mary and Joseph.

At the start of the Gospel of John, Jesus is identified as God's Word made flesh who "made his dwelling among us" (1:14) In ancient times, God dwelled with his people in the desert tabernacle and then in the Jerusalem temple, where only very few were allowed to approach God's presence in the Holy of Holies. In Jesus, God dwells among all people as a human being.

Paul echoes this remarkable development when he writes that "though he was in the form of God, / [Jesus] did not regard equality with God something to be grasped." Instead, he "emptied himself" to be filled with humanity (Phil 2:6-7). In today's Gospel Jesus tells us he wants us to be filled with divinity, God's very life, and to dwell where he dwells for eternity.

Human beings are not treated as an experiment by God or a test for God's Son. Rather, we are a product of God's love and an extension of God's presence in the world, and so we will enjoy dwelling with God for eternity.

Jesus reminds his followers that he is not teaching a philosophy or proposing one more truth for us to study. Jesus himself *is* the way, *is* the truth, and *is* the life that we seek to live.

**Meditation:** The very idea that God dwells with us in Jesus so we can dwell with him for all time gives us pause. To dwell is to linger, to abide, or to take up residence. One who dwells is committed to more than a quick visit. God, who dwells with us in Jesus, takes in everything about the human experience and continues to walk with us through it all.

**Prayer:** Good and gracious Shepherd, help us desire to be with you as much as you have committed to dwell with us.

## Believing What We See

**Readings:** Acts 13:44-52; John 14:7-14

**Scripture:**
All the ends of the earth have seen the saving power of God.
(Ps 98:3)

**Reflection:** Several weeks ago, as we began the Easter season, we pondered together why some who saw the risen Jesus did not believe. Today's readings bring us to this question once again. In the Gospel reading from John, the apostles who are gathered at the Last Supper are slow to catch on, still unsure whether Jesus is the Son of God. The scene from Acts reflects the period after Jesus' ascension, when many rejected the apostles' message about the resurrection of Jesus.

The psalmist proclaims, "All the ends of the earth have seen the saving power of God." So all have seen God at work, but perhaps not all are aware of what they are seeing. If we wish to know the power of God in our world, we must be humble enough to set aside any rigid thinking that would prevent our *sight* from becoming *insight*. We must be willing to look at our surroundings as if we've just gotten new lenses for our glasses. Do we see only what is occurring on the surface or do we look more deeply? Are we able to recognize when goodness is growing even if the "soil" that is producing the good doesn't seem to be an obvious place for growth?

Are we willing to let God be God rather than molding God in our own image or according to our own preferences?

The saving power of God is not limited to rare occasions of the miraculous. God's power is evident in things we take for granted, like the wonders of nature and the ways our bodies change through the seasons of our lives. It is found in simple acts of service as well as profound moments of self-sacrifice. God's power appears when reconciliation replaces revenge, restoration replaces punishment, and justice is afforded to the oppressed or forgotten.

**Meditation:** While God's power may at times appear overwhelming, it is most often *under*whelming, sometimes barely noticeable, when compared with typical political and economic power. In your experience, how does God exercise power in ways that are unexpected?

**Prayer:** Good and gracious Shepherd, open our eyes to see you and our hearts to know you.

## Disciples Love One Another

**Readings:** Acts 14:21-27; Rev 21:1-5a; John 13:31-33a, 34-35

**Scripture:**
"This is how all will know that you are my disciples, if you have love for one another." (John 13:35)

**Reflection:** I remember watching a heated (and then over-heated) debate develop at a parish meeting and thinking to myself, "If this is how we treat each other right here in our own parish where we share common values, no wonder we have trouble showing love to people whose values are completely different than our own." But then again, maybe it's easier to act lovingly to people we don't know!

Today's Gospel scene occurs just after Jesus has washed the feet of his disciples as they gather for their last meal together. I can't help but wonder what would have happened at our parish meeting had someone in leadership quietly filled a bowl with water, grabbed a towel, and started washing feet. I'm serious! With our socks and shoes removed, totally un-prepared for this ritual, we would all have been on common ground, reduced as it were, to pairs of dirty feet. I have a feeling it would have stripped away the anger and helped us reason together in a more loving and respectful way.

In these hours before Jesus is arrested, he is still concerned with his divine mission to demonstrate God's love to all people. His disciples will only be able to bear witness to him, to welcome others into their community, insofar as they demonstrate love among themselves: respectfully honest with one another, quick to forgive, generous in service, and joyful in their common faith.

**Meditation:** Flight attendants begin each flight with safety announcements, including instructions to put on your oxygen mask first before helping others do the same in an emergency. It's not a selfish act; it's essential and practical. Could showing love to others in our faith communities be likened to that procedure? Can we work on loving each other there first so that we are then able to witness effectively to others that our God is love?

**Prayer:** Jesus, you command us to love as you love. Give us this day the determination to be generous in our relationships with fellow parishioners.

## **Recognizing Our Idols**

**Readings:** Acts 14:5-18; John 14:21-26

**Scripture:**
"We proclaim to you good news that you should turn from these idols to the living God, *who made heaven and earth and sea and all that is in them.*" (Acts 14:15)

**Reflection:** I think most of us are quick to associate idolatry with pagan worship practices. The Canaanites worshipped Baal among others, the Greeks and Romans had their pantheons of gods, and the Romans went so far as to worship the emperor as a god. Even in modern cultures, political leaders are sometimes the object of worship. Psalm 135 bemoans the idols that are mere statues, with eyes that cannot see and mouths that cannot speak. Paul and Barnabas call the people in Lystra to turn from idols to worship the living God, the God who is actively engaged in creation and redemption.

But in the biblical tradition, idolatry is much broader than pagan worship. The prophets of Israel and Judah portrayed God's relationship or covenant with us as a marriage, so allegiance to any kind of false gods can be considered adultery. This intimate description of our relationship with God might cause us to squirm a bit. If we seek our ultimate fulfillment by trusting or desiring anything more than God, that is idolatry. What are our false gods? Are we willing to acknowledge them? How are we being called toward worship of the living God?

For some of us the culprit is maintaining a certain reputation. For others it might be vanity, popularity on social media, achieving a certain income level, using alcohol or drugs to avoid responsibility, or gambling. Self-examination can reveal where we are most in need of a fresh commitment to seek first God's kingdom, to worship only the God of creation and redemption.

**Meditation:** Where do I invest the treasure of my time? The treasure of my financial resources? The treasure of my heart? Do I seek God's will in how I use my time, money, and devotion? Jesus promises in today's Gospel that he will send the Spirit to teach and remind us of everything we need. Each day we can ask the Spirit to direct our devotion toward the living God.

**Prayer:** Jesus, you command us to love as you love. Help us to put loving you above all else, so we may recognize where you are leading us and how you would have us spend the treasure of our lives.

## **Persistence Born of Friendship**

**Readings:** Acts 14:19-28; John 14:27-31a

**Scripture:**
Your friends make known, O Lord, the glorious splendor of
your kingdom. (Ps 145:12)

**Reflection:** On this day, the church has selected Psalm 145
as a response to our reading from Acts and as a prelude of
sorts to our Gospel reading, which is a portion of Jesus' Last
Supper discourse in John's Gospel. If we're reading or listening carefully, it might seem almost ironic to extol the splen-
dors of God's kingdom between two readings that sound a
bittersweet note.

Paul barely escapes death in the scene from Acts; then he
and Barnabas tell the church in Antioch about the necessity
of undergoing hardships to enter the kingdom of God. And
in the Gospel, Jesus tries to prepare his followers for the realities they will face, acknowledging that they will be troubled
and afraid, and that he will be away for a while but will return.
Both readings avoid the trap of focusing only on the "glory"
side of evangelizing. The harsh reality is that resistance to the
Good News is uncomfortable and can even be dangerous.

But Jesus, the apostles, and even the psalmist never lose
sight of their goal, and they persist in proclaiming the good
that God is doing. When we pray Psalm 145, we are not

ignoring the reality of hardship or the cost of laboring for the kingdom. Instead, we are reminding ourselves of the deep truth that God has called us friends, and that the kingdom of God is not beyond our reach. Our friendship with God and the deep sense of peace we are given will equip us for whatever lies ahead.

**Meditation:** The stories of the apostles traveling throughout the Mediterranean region sometimes sound like an action movie. The apostles never seem to grow weary, nor do they waver in their convictions about Jesus. Wouldn't you like to have been a fly on the wall late at night when they no doubt shared with God their weariness and fears? What gave them—and what gives us—the ability to persist?

**Prayer:** Jesus, you command us to love as you love. Give us the grace of your friendship and the gift of peace even when our efforts land us in deep waters that threaten to engulf us.

## **Producing the Fruit of the Vine**

**Readings:** Acts 15:1-6; John 15:1-8

**Scripture:**
"Remain in me, as I remain in you. Just as a branch cannot bear fruit on its own unless it remains on the vine, so neither can you unless you remain in me." (John 15:4)

**Reflection:** Partly because they thrived in the region, vines and vineyards became a symbolic way to speak about ancient Israel in their tradition. The prophet Hosea compared Israel to a luxuriant vine and then bemoaned how the plentiful harvest led to the worship of false gods (10:1). Similarly, Jeremiah said Israel was planted as a choice vine that turned out to be obnoxious and spurious (2:21). The whole of Psalm 80 is a plea for God to restore Israel, a vine that was brought from Egypt and filled the land with fruit.

In the Gospel of John, Jesus takes up this image and speaks of himself as the "true vine" whose growth will not be corrupted or thwarted. Vines and branches become the perfect analogy for speaking of how important it is to remain or abide in Christ and to allow Christ to remain or abide in us. The vine provides the roots and nutrients needed for growth, and the branches provide fruit that in turn strengthens the entire plant. Vines and branches share a mutual or symbiotic relationship, like that of Jesus and his followers.

Macrina Wiederkehr, OSB, speaks of abiding or remaining as "keeping vigil," a beautiful way to picture the tender devotion of Jesus, who watches and waits with us as we grow and produce fruit. And we too keep vigil with Jesus, listening and watching for the instruction we need to nurture us and the commitment we need to grow and produce the fruit that will nourish others.

**Meditation:** Jesus asks that we bear much fruit and become his disciples. Where do you look for the fruit produced in your life by remaining or abiding with Jesus? Are there people you trust who can help you discern the kind of fruit you are producing as a result of remaining in Christ?

**Prayer:** Jesus, you command us to love as you love. From our love for you, produce fruit that is lasting and tangible, fruit that feeds those who are hungry for the rootedness you provide.

## Joy Cannot Be Stolen

**Readings:** Acts 15:7-21; John 15:9-11

**Scripture:**
"Remain in my love. . . .
I have told you this so that my joy might be in you and your
joy might be complete." (John 15:9, 11)

**Reflection:** I can vividly recall being at a conference many
years ago where the speaker asked a very large crowd of us
if we believed that the Gospel is "good news." When we
yelled back with a resounding "Yes," he said, "Then tell your
face about it!" The hardships that come with discipleship
cannot erase the joy of discipleship.

Henri Nouwen, one of the great spiritual writers of the
late twentieth century, said that joy doesn't just happen to
us but is something we choose: "It is a choice based on the
knowledge that we belong to God and have found in God
our refuge and our safety and that nothing, not even death,
can take God away from us." In other words, the joy of Christians is not simply an emotional reaction. It is steeped in
God's love for us and spills over into our love for others.
Nouwen, transparent about his own spiritual and emotional
struggles, knew this love and joy deeply from his own experience, especially in his final years living in a L'Arche community outside of Toronto. There he served as a chaplain,

caregiver, and friend to the mixed community of people with and without intellectual and physical challenges.

In our own daily routines, we choose joy because we know the love of God, but what about those times when God's love does not feel real or tangible, when we feel distant from God? My advice is simple: in these times let's choose joy anyway, and we will surely rediscover God's abiding love.

**Meditation:** Dorothy Day, the American journalist, peace activist, and co-founder of the Catholic Worker movement, knew the challenges of working for social change through the lens of the Gospel. Her work with the poor and oppressed was serious business. And yet she said Christians are called to the "duty of delight." How are you making room for joy and delight in your witness to the Gospel?

**Prayer:** Jesus, you command us to love as you love. May the love we show to others be saturated with the joy of finding you present in every person we encounter.

# Who Is Seeking Who?

**Readings:** Acts 15:22-31; John 15:12-17

**Scripture:**
"It was not you who chose me, but I who chose you and appointed you to go and bear fruit that will remain." (John 15:16)

**Reflection:** For most of my life I saw the Bible's characters, as well as canonized saints and other holy people, as seeking and then finding God. Doesn't Isaiah tell Israel, "Seek the LORD while he may be found, / call upon him while he is near" (55:6)? And doesn't Jeremiah promise God's people that they will find God if they seek with their whole heart (29:13)? Even Jesus tells his followers to seek the kingdom of God (Matt 6:33).

However (and this is a good "however"!), so much of what we read in our Bibles and in Christian history clearly shows that it is actually *God* who is always seeking *us*. Moses wasn't looking for God; God was looking for him and even set a bush on fire to get his attention. Not a single one of the biblical prophets was out seeking God (or a new mission for that matter), but God found them and commissioned them in the midst of their daily routines. Mary wasn't seeking God or asking for any favors, but God found favor with her and sought her out to bear his Son. Both the prophet Ezekiel and

Jesus tell us that God, the Good Shepherd, searches for his people, his sheep.

It is humbling to know that the Creator of the universe is not only willing but eager in seeking us out. It simply takes a spirit of openness to God's presence for us to hear God's call. And even a hesitant "yes" in response gives God the opportunity to put us to work, to "go and bear fruit" that will last.

**Meditation:** Where do you feel that God is choosing to call you at this time in your life? Are you willing to say "yes"? If not, why might you be hesitating? Ask God to give you the courage to go where God leads and do what you can.

**Prayer:** Jesus, you command us to love as you love. Open the eyes and ears of our hearts so we recognize your call, and give us the humility to say "yes" to what you would have each of us do for you.

## Facing Life Head On

**Reading:** Acts 16:1-10; John 15:18-21

**Scripture:**
"If they persecuted me, they will also persecute you. If they kept my word, they will also keep yours." (John 15:20)

**Reflection:** Do you feel like you're on a bit of a roller coaster ride this week? Both persecution and joy seem to be popping up every other day. Perhaps that's the way it is with daily life—one day we have the world by its tail, and the next day we feel the world has beaten us down. Jesus was no stranger to these rhythms of what it means to be human, taking the bad with the good. And Jesus helps us find meaning in both.

By telling his disciples that they will suffer as he did and be trusted as he was, Jesus is saying something along the lines of: "That's how closely I am with you, and that's how your life is bound up in mine. When people see you, they see me also." His words were meant to remind the disciples that he is not immune to suffering and that they should expect nothing less themselves. His words also encourage and assure them that they have a share in his power and authority, especially among the faithful.

I had a bad fall a few years ago while on my way into a building where a Scripture study group was waiting to hear me speak. I was out of commission for a while, having broken multiple bones in and around my face. The people in that group were so good to me as I recovered, and I recall one of them saying that because I was doing God's work, I shouldn't have been hurt; it just wasn't fair. How often we want Christianity to be like a magic wand that waves the bad away from every follower of Jesus! But Christianity asks us to deal with hard things head on, just as Jesus did.

**Meditation:** Life presents us with so many opportunities to respond to situations as Jesus would. Where are you finding such opportunities in your life in these Easter days?

**Prayer:** Jesus, you command us to love as you love. Help us to embrace the human condition as Jesus embraced it.

## Facing New Possibilities

**Readings:** Acts 15:1-2, 22-29; Rev 21:10-14, 22-23; John 14:23-29

**Scripture:**
"It is the decision of the Holy Spirit and of us not to place on you any burden beyond these necessities . . ." (Acts 15:28)

**Reflection:** The first Christians or followers of Jesus the Christ were Jewish. It's easy to lose sight of that when so much of the New Testament was written as his followers were preaching in new territories, eventually becoming a separate entity from Judaism. Even Paul's earliest letters, written before the first Gospel, exhibit traces of the tensions that were growing between traditional sects of Judaism and this newest sect, whose members believed that Jesus was the long-awaited Messiah.

The readings from Acts this week follow the missionary efforts of some of the apostles beyond the familiar borders of Israel and Judaism. Initially they seek out Jewish enclaves across the region, but soon enough Gentiles are responding to the apostles' message and requesting baptism. Leaders of the early church convened in Jerusalem to hear what was happening in the mission field and to determine how to proceed with regard to Gentile converts. Must they become

Jews first in order to become members of the Christian community? Or is faith in Jesus, itself a gift, enough to "qualify" Gentiles as true believers and full-fledged members of the church?

The decision of the Council was sent around the region: becoming Jewish was not necessary for becoming Christian. What is of particular importance in this account is that this momentous decision came from the Holy Spirit and the church. Jesus did not leave specific instructions about this inevitable development among Gentiles, but he did promise that the Spirit would assist his followers. This early decision of the emerging church is a profound example of how doctrine and practice would continue to take shape across the centuries.

**Meditation:** When the church or individual Christians are faced with difficult decisions, we have two companion routes to help us get to a resolution. The first route is to offer our concerns, ideas, and efforts to the Spirit to help guide us. The second is to do the hard work of gathering information and carefully considering options. How could this two-part process help assure a healthy response when we are uncertain about something?

**Prayer:** O God, it is your will to draw all people to yourself. May our decisions on the local and international levels reflect what tradition teaches us and what the Spirit guides us to understand.

## Discipleship and Hospitality

**Readings:** Acts 16:11-15; John 15:26–16:4a

**Scripture:**
After [Lydia] and her household had been baptized, she offered us an invitation, "If you consider me a believer in the Lord, come and stay at my home," and she prevailed on us. (Acts 16:15)

**Reflection:** Silas and Paul's arrival in Philippi led to the establishment of the first Christian community in what is now Europe. It is said that Lydia, a woman of some means, was initially the head of the church that was established there, inviting the community into her home to break open the Word and to break bread together.

But before all that, Lydia was among the women who were at the river when the missionaries first arrived. We might see some parallels here with the Gospel scene of Jesus and the Samaritan woman at the well. In both cases, it is unusual for men to be conversing in public with women; in both stories, the women are deeply engaged in the discussion; and finally, both encounters lead to apparent outsiders accepting that Jesus is indeed the Messiah and Son of God.

Accepting Jesus in baptism as Lydia did is not the end of her story but merely the beginning. The first thing Lydia does is offer hospitality to Silas and Paul. Just as they opened the story of Jesus for her, now she opens her home to them. We see in the brief description of their encounter that the hospitality each offered was not mere custom but an expression of their shared faith.

This community in Philippi continued to offer generous financial and prayerful support for Paul's missionary activity. It is therefore not a surprise that Paul's letter to the Philippians is among the most joyful of all his writing.

**Meditation:** Imagine what it might have been like for the women gathered at the river as these unknown travelers approached them. Perhaps because of safety in numbers they felt at ease speaking to the men and hearing their story. Lydia was receptive to their message because "the Lord opened her heart to pay attention." May we too have such a heart.

**Prayer:** O God, it is your will to draw all people to yourself. Help us imitate the apostles and look for opportunities to share with others the wonders of your love.

## A Transforming Earthquake

**Readings:** Acts 16:22-34; John 16:5-11

**Scripture:**
[The jailer] took them in at that hour of the night and bathed their wounds; then he and all his family were baptized at once. (Acts 16:33)

**Reflection:** In Philippi, Paul and Silas heal a young slave who was being used by her owners as a fortune-teller. Once healed of her infirmity (possession by a spirit, according to Acts), her owners realize they can no longer profit from her. They rail against Paul and Silas and have them arrested. Both men are beaten and put into an innermost prison cell where their feet are chained to a stake.

For all the precautions taken to prevent the prisoners' escape, while they are at prayer that night, a strong earthquake shakes the jail so severely that the prison doors open and their chains are broken apart. The guard is ready to kill himself, believing he failed to secure the prisoners, but both Paul and Silas call out to assure him they are still there. In a wonderful reversal, the jailer humbles himself before the two missionaries, asking how he can be saved.

The jailer who was ready to kill himself in shame is now anxious to take the prisoners to his home to bathe their wounds. Like Lydia, the jailer opens the door to faith through hospitality. Doing his duty for the empire becomes relative to serving the needs of God's messengers. Believing in the justice of imperial law is now a distant second to believing in God. Perhaps even more to the point, the kind of faith that leads the jailer and his household to baptism is more akin to trust than intellectual assent. They have come to know and trust God through an experience of human kindness rather than through an explanation of doctrine. Isn't this how God often works?

**Meditation:** Hopefully most of us will never experience the terror of an actual earthquake. But there are moments in our lives that can feel like a spiritual earthquake. When an event or series of events overturns our view of the world, it's time to get on our knees and ask God to strip away our attachment to false securities and lead us to what is true and lasting.

**Prayer:** O God, it is your will to draw all people to yourself. Just as you used the forces of nature to awaken faith within the jailer in Philippi, use your power to wake us from complacency.

## Preaching in New Worlds

**Readings:** Acts 17:15, 22–18:1; John 16:12-15

**Scripture:**
"The God who made the world and all that is in it . . . fixed the ordered seasons and the boundaries of their regions, so that people might seek God, even perhaps grope for him and find him, though indeed he is not far from any one of us." (Acts 17:24, 26-27)

**Reflection:** The Good News of Jesus is steady, unchanging, and true. However, how that Good News is preached must take into account the various cultures where it is proclaimed. What are the interests and values of a particular people? How do they express themselves publicly and privately? How does their language function? Across the centuries, the most effective and lasting methods of evangelization have shown great sensitivity to unique peoples and cultures.

Evangelization cannot be reduced to learning a script to be used in all circumstances. Rather, evangelization is about forging relationships between people, authentic relationships that introduce and embody the God we know and wish to share with others.

When Paul arrives in Athens, the intellectual center of the Roman Empire, he tries a very different way of drawing people to the Good News than he typically employed among fellow Jews, or among Gentiles in more isolated regions. These Athenians are people whose culture is immersed in both religion and philosophy. They are interested in hearing new ideas and are actively searching for meaning. Paul recognizes that he can use this natural religious inclination and pursuit of meaning to introduce them to the true God who gives meaning to all creation. Hoping to draw them to want to hear more, he preaches using the expansive intellectual language of philosophy and poetry rather than the religious language of monotheistic Judaism.

Those who impose their own culture as part and parcel of the Christian message do a disservice to the Gospel and to the people who are being evangelized. Those who immerse themselves in the lives of the people they encounter are better able to preach and teach the Gospel in a way that resonates and truly takes hold.

**Meditation:** If you are unfamiliar with some of the missionary efforts of contemporary Christians, seek out information on such people as Blessed Stanley Rother, who served in Guatemala, or Fr. Gregory Boyle and Homeboy Industries, currently active among gangs in the Los Angeles area. They learned to speak the cultural language of the people they love and serve.

**Prayer:** O God, it is your will to draw all people to yourself. Give us the grace to meet people in their own circumstances before giving voice to what we wish to share.

## Out of Kilter

**Readings:** Acts 18:1-8; John 16:16-20 (or Acts 1:1-11; Eph 1:17-23 or Heb 9:24-28; 10:19-23; Luke 24:46-53)

**Scripture:**
"Amen, amen, I say to you, you will weep and mourn, while the world rejoices; you will grieve, but your grief will become joy." (John 16:20)

**Reflection:** Have you ever felt like you sensed something that others did not? Or perhaps you sometimes feel disoriented by the world around you, as if you are out of step. That's not necessarily a bad thing. As Christians, it is not unusual to be out of sync with the dominant culture; in fact, Christianity is often countercultural.

In today's Gospel, the risen Jesus is preparing his followers for the time when he will not be physically present among them. He knows it will be disorienting and that they will not feel at ease with much that will be swirling around them. Jesus' reassurance includes the promise that they will see him again and that the Spirit will dwell with them.

In John 16, we see the cycle of what biblical scholar Walter Brueggemann calls "orientation, disorientation, and reorientation." The closest followers of Jesus seem to be just getting into the rhythm of discipleship when Jesus is arrested and crucified. Their world then collapses in many ways. Their hopes for his role as Messiah are dashed, but they will be called to a deeper understanding when they meet the risen Lord. Similarly, after the resurrection, they surely feel a renewed hope only to be told that Jesus will be returning to the Father. Their time of disorientation will lead once again to a deeper understanding of how Jesus remains with them through the Spirit.

This cycle is not a quick process. In fact, in some ways we are still dealing with the disorientation of having a Messiah who suffers, but we live in hope that our own suffering will lead to the total reorientation of new life in Christ.

**Meditation:** When we feel out of sync with the world around us, what might God be doing within us? Are our false securities coming to light? Are we becoming complacent with the way things are and need to be reminded that the kingdom of God is utterly different from this world?

**Prayer:** O God, it is your will to draw all people to yourself. Be with us when we are muddling our way through crisis or doubt, and give us the sure footing of walking with you.

## Joy in Friendship

**Readings:** Acts 18:9-18; John 16:20-23

**Scripture:**
"I will see you again, and your hearts will rejoice, and no one will take your joy away from you." (John 16:22)

**Reflection:** I have a dear friend in Australia, literally on the other side of the globe from me. Another dear friend is in Canada, and my college roommate is in Wisconsin. While we occasionally talk by phone or email, I have not seen any of these friends in person in quite some time. I miss them. I miss cups of tea with long and meaningful conversations. I miss spending time in their presence and the laughter we always share. I think of each of these women on a daily basis, and in my prayer, I thank God for their steadfast presence even in their physical absence. They live in my heart as gifts that keep on giving.

As I'm learning to watercolor, I think of Pat and her artistic spirit. Not only did my roommate dwell in creativity that influences me still, but she gave me a deeper appreciation for St. Francis, who she emulates. Dorian shows me how to live in strength and in tenderness; she faces every reality with both qualities. And Jan? Jan is present with me when I read the Scriptures because her life embodies them so well. I know I will see each of them again in this world or the next, and that deepens the joy I have when I think of them or pray for them.

Among the apostles, Jesus proves himself to be a master teacher, a healer, and a savior. Perhaps best of all, Jesus is their friend who lives in their hearts until they meet again. What a joyful reunion! They will recognize him because of the countless ways he has stayed alive and present to them even in his physical absence.

**Meditation:** When we call to mind the gift of friendship and the friends whose spirits abide with us even when we are apart, we catch a glimpse of the friendship Jesus offers to us. When do you feel his presence with you? How does friendship with Jesus sustain you? Compel you forward? Give you joy?

**Prayer:** O God, it is your will to draw all people to yourself. You have given us your friendship through Jesus, as a gift to enliven our hearts and a hope that brings us joy.

## **Faithful Listening to the *Magnificat***

**Readings:** Zeph 3:14-18a or Rom 12:9-16; Luke 1:39-56

**Scripture:**
"My soul proclaims the greatness of the Lord; / my spirit rejoices in God my Savior, / for he has looked with favor on his lowly servant. / From this day all generations will call me blessed: / the Almighty has done great things for me, / and holy is his Name." (Luke 1:46-49)

**Reflection:** I think we can agree that most Catholics are exposed to Scripture primarily through the readings at Mass on Sundays. What a shame that the Canticle of Mary (or *Magnificat*) does not appear as a Sunday Gospel in the normal cycle of readings! It is the Gospel reading for the Assumption of Mary, a holy day of obligation, but our churches are rarely filled on such days. And while the *Magnificat* is part of the Liturgy of the Hours, most lay Catholics do not use this prayer form regularly. We seem to be missing out on a profound Scripture passage that some have called "the Gospel in miniature."

Without regular exposure to this prayer on the lips of Mary, I fear that we miss the deeply transformative experience of Mary's pregnancy, not just for her but for the entire world. She begins her prayer by focusing on what God has done for her, but that is not where she lingers. Instead, Mary shifts her prayer to proclaim the mercy of God for all people and describes the complete reversal of the world's priorities: the proud are scattered, the mighty lose their power, and the rich discover the empty promise of wealth, while the lowly are lifted up, and the hungry are filled with good things. Years later, these same themes will be echoed in the life and ministry of Jesus.

In the safety of Elizabeth's home, two pregnant women share their joys and hopes, and perhaps their fears. This setting provides the perfect backdrop for a prayer that embraces hope for a kingdom that is unlike any other.

**Meditation:** Make time today to prayerfully read Luke 1:39-56. Picture the joy of Elizabeth as she greets Mary. Listen for the humility of Mary, and her brave proclamation that God welcomes all but is particularly close to the lowly and forgotten. How might you become more aware of your own lowliness and God's closeness with you?

**Prayer:** O God, it is your will to draw all people to yourself. Help us discover the hungers that only you can fill in us. May we be counted among the lowly.

*June 1: The Ascension of the Lord*
*(or Seventh Sunday of Easter)*

## Gazing Over Jerusalem

**Readings:** Acts 1:1-11; Eph 1:17-23 or Heb 9:24-28; 10:19-23; Luke 24:46-53 (or Acts 7:55-60; Rev 22:12-14, 16-17, 20; John 17:20-26)

**Scripture:**
Then [Jesus] led them out as far as Bethany, raised his hands, and blessed them. As he blessed them he parted from them and was taken up to heaven. They did him homage and then returned to Jerusalem with great joy. (Luke 24:50-52)

**Reflection:** There is a very simple chapel, really more of a shrine, on the hillside just outside Jerusalem that memorializes the ascension of the Lord. From this site, pilgrims can see the city of Jerusalem and picture in their minds how the risen Lord would have looked upon the sacred city as he ascended back to God.

As the site of Jesus' death and resurrection, Jerusalem represented for the disciples both death and life, great sadness and utter joy. In this life, there is no escaping either end of the spectrum. The response of the disciples to Jesus' return to his Father demonstrates the necessity of holding both realities, searching for meaning in both heartbreak and elation. We might assume the disciples would be left with a bittersweet taste in their mouths as Jesus departs, but today's

Gospel tells us their response is joy, and that rather than flee the city, they remain there praising God in the temple. It is quite a reversal from cowering in an Upper Room after Jesus' crucifixion, fearful and in disbelief.

I would guess that all of us have our "Jerusalems"—places or times that we associate with the mixed bag of surviving deep sorrow or wrestling with unforeseen disappointment. It is in the surviving and the wrestling that we just might discover healing and the renewal of hope. Just as the disciples of Jesus could finally let him go and rediscover Jerusalem as a spiritual home, we too might find hope and comfort in our own Jerusalems.

**Meditation:** The ascension of Jesus is as much about developing as disciples as it is about Jesus completing his earthly mission. All these centuries later, we are still learning what it means to be the Body of Christ on earth, to continue to bear witness to Jesus and be part of proclaiming the kingdom of God. While we will always be children of God, we must mature into adult disciples, relying on the Spirit to clothe us with the wisdom we need to face the world with the same joy as the first disciples.

**Prayer:** Spirit of the Living God, refresh us. Allow us to stay close to Jesus without clinging so we can mature into the kind of disciples Jesus wants and the world needs.

## The Necessity of the Spirit

**Readings:** Acts 19:1-8; John 16:29-33

**Scripture:**
[Paul] said to them, "Did you receive the Holy Spirit when you became believers?" They answered him, "We have never even heard that there is a Holy Spirit." (Acts 19:2)

**Reflection:** Sometimes we assume that the beliefs and practices we now hold dear as Christians were evident from the very beginning of the church's history. However, an attentive reading of the New Testament tells us that the earliest generations of believers had much to sort out: the acceptance of Gentiles and what that meant for Jesus' followers and their ongoing relationship to Judaism, the shape of liturgy as Christianity spread from place to place, and even the formula and significance of baptism, as we see in our reading today from Acts.

As with any new movement, the fervor of the initial stages outweighs the necessity of pinning down the particulars. The early Christians were also contending with how to even keep up with what God was doing with their efforts! Small communities of believers were emerging quickly as missionaries fanned out in the region from Jerusalem to Rome. Commissioned and non-commissioned believers spread the Good News of Jesus to a population hungry for rich and nourishing messages of hope and for teachings that embodied the truth.

Along the way, some who were baptized had not been told about or experienced the Spirit as part of their baptismal ritual (see also Acts 8:15-17). But for Paul and for Luke, the author of Acts, it is impossible to live in and for Christ without the Spirit. It is the Spirit of God who descends on Jesus at his own baptism, and on the apostles gathered in Jerusalem after Jesus' resurrection. It is the Spirit who binds together believers in every generation, all the while inviting us to open the door to new experiences of God at work among us.

**Meditation:** We believe the Spirit of God is at work in the formation and refinement of the church's teachings. At the same time, we know the Spirit is not finished with us or with deepening our appreciation for God's always expanding mercy. When we ask the Spirit to inhabit our days, we are asking that God's will be done in and through us.

**Prayer:** Spirit of the Living God, refresh us. Help us to trust that you are always at work in us, renewing our baptismal identity.

## Eternal Life

**Readings:** Acts 20:17-27; John 17:1-11a

**Scripture:**
"Now this is eternal life, that they [all people] should know you, the only true God, and the one whom you sent, Jesus Christ." (John 17:3)

**Reflection:** I'll wager that many of us have spent quite a bit of time over the course of our lives wondering about the eternal life that we believe awaits us. As a child I thought of it as a faraway heaven, and I pictured the perfect playground and fried chicken at the ready. In my tweens when my grandpa died, I pictured more of a throne room that he would be welcome to enter. A little later, I was focused on the picture of Jesus going to prepare a place for us, one of the many dwelling places or even mansions in his Father's house. I understood these images very literally into early adulthood.

As I've experienced more deaths of those I love, and more of a sense that life itself is sacred, I'm not so worried about what heaven will look like, as if it is a place that can be identified by its decor. Heaven is not simply a faraway place, and eternal life is not something that begins only after death. In John's Gospel, Jesus is inviting us to begin experiencing eternal life right here in our own backyards. He tells us that eternal life is knowing the only true God: *knowing* God, not simply knowing *about* God.

Eternal life is experienced in relationship with the God who fashioned us in the womb, the God who walks with us even when we are unaware, the God who corrects and redirects us, the God who sends his Son and gifts us with human relationships that become part of the fabric of our being. Jesus teaches his followers about eternal life in the midst of a world that rejects him and will reject them. Eternal life is not a reward for good behavior; it is simply the gift of the most precious relationship we will ever know.

**Meditation:** When we direct our hopes toward knowing God in an intimate and real way, we catch glimpses of eternal life all around us.

**Prayer:** Spirit of the Living God, refresh us. In our yearnings to find a world unlike this one or to reunite with loved ones who have died, remind us that anything we can imagine will be surpassed by truly coming to know you.

## Spiritual Refueling

**Readings:** Acts 20:28-38; John 17:11b-19

**Scripture:**
"As you sent me into the world, so I sent them into the world." (John 17:18)

**Reflection:** Have you ever wondered about your purpose in the world? I've certainly had moments when I felt I needed clarity. Such moments might come in times of crisis when we wonder if we're up to the task ahead of us. Even in the humdrum of our daily routines it's easy to become complacent or melancholy, even a bit rudderless.

A friend recently asked me, "What am I really here for, anyway? Am I actually contributing to the world?" We've been friends for a long time, so, after listening a while, I was able to share with him how I feel he makes a difference. A few days later I went back to him and said simply, "Jesus sent you into this world at this time and in this place—he's the one you should be asking!" I think he needed some spiritual refueling, and he agreed. In fact, it wouldn't hurt any of us to be reminded that God brought us here, Jesus has sent us out, and the Spirit is accompanying us.

The fact that God chooses to work in this world through *us* is breathtaking. We may have chosen a different way to save the world or initiate the kingdom of God, but surely

God's wisdom is greater than ours. The doubts we may have about being empowered by God to continue Christ's mission are cause for prayer. As we draw closer to God, even to express our inadequacies or admit our complacency, we are reminded that we are on a divine mission. We will not waste our lives but will spend them wisely if we allow God to work through us.

**Meditation:** When have another person's words or deeds given evidence that they are on a mission from God? Even the smallest act can become an avenue of grace-filled encounter and a reminder that God is at work in our very midst. Where might God be sending you to bring his presence this day?

**Prayer:** Spirit of the Living God, refresh us. Remind us of your purpose for our lives and of Jesus' promise to help us bear witness to truth.

## Knowing How to Love

**Readings:** Acts 22:30; 23:6-11; John 17:20-26

**Scripture:**
"Father, they are your gift to me." (John 17:24)

**Reflection:** When Jesus prays in the hours before his death, he calls his followers—perhaps his closest followers—God's gift to him.

I am not doubting for a moment that Jesus believed deeply in the goodness of those who traveled with him during his ministry, shared meals with him, sometimes tried to protect him, and always stayed close to him. But I am reminded of a scene from the Gospel of Matthew where a man presents his son for healing and reports to Jesus that his disciples could not effect a cure or an exorcism. The exasperated response of Jesus helps us to imagine him rolling his eyes in disbelief, or shaking his head in disappointment in his disciples: "O faithless and perverse generation, how long will I be with you? How long will I endure you?" (Matt 17:17). Talk about a scene that highlights the humanity of Jesus!

Jesus expects more of those who are closest to him and at times becomes exasperated with them, much like we might sometimes feel about our children or a trusted colleague. But, of course, these moments of exasperation do not erase the love and concern we have for those close to us, or that Jesus had for his followers.

Jesus schooled his disciples in the qualities of divinity, stretching them to trust in a Messiah and a kingdom that were quite different from their expectations. Likewise, the disciples provided a school of humanity for him, helping Jesus see where compassion and patience were most needed. In the fullness of his humanity, Jesus assuredly valued the disciples both for their experiences and for their own worthiness.

**Meditation:** Christians have often emphasized either the divine Jesus or the human Jesus, as if they are separate experiences. It's awfully challenging to understand that Jesus is at once fully divine and fully human, as we profess in our creed. Perhaps it's best to set aside a preoccupation with explaining the two natures of Jesus and simply take the leap of embracing Jesus as he embraces us, even with all our foibles.

**Prayer:** Spirit of the Living God, refresh us. Help us to believe that Jesus embraces us as gifts from God, not because we are perfect but because he knows how to love.

## Feed My Sheep

**Readings:** Acts 25:13b-21; John 21:15-19

**Scripture:**
Peter was distressed that [Jesus] had said to him a third time,
"Do you love me?" and he said to him, "Lord, you know
everything; you know that I love you." Jesus said to him,
"Feed my sheep." (John 21:17)

**Reflection:** Along the northwestern shore of the Sea of Tiberias (or Sea of Galilee), at a place known as Tabgha, there is
a life-size sculpture commemorating the encounter of Peter
with the Risen Lord. Located near the shoreline, it is striking
in its simplicity, with Peter kneeling before Jesus, his hand
lifted and open as Jesus extends his hand over the man who,
just days earlier, had denied him. In Jesus' darkest hour,
Peter had failed to be near Jesus or even admit knowing him.
Now Peter is given the opportunity to express in words what
he should have said earlier: that he not only knows Jesus but
loves him. Perhaps even more importantly, Peter is instructed
to put his words into action as Jesus tells him: "Feed my
sheep."

Love cannot exist in a vacuum. It requires mutual relationship and must take shape in our actions. Jesus demonstrated
this reality time and again in his ministry. He engaged with
people in need and with people who did not know their

need. He healed and shared meals, and sometimes miraculously fed multitudes with very little food. Poignantly, Tabgha is also the place that memorializes Jesus feeding the crowds with simple loaves and fish. On that day Jesus had already fed the crowd with teaching that was challenging and hope-filled, but he knew their stomachs needed nourishment too.

Jesus was telling Peter—and telling all who profess to love Jesus, especially leaders—that love carries with it a responsibility. Love is not a feeling nearly as much as it is a decision to nourish those around us, to strengthen individuals and communities by meeting the most basic human needs of mind, body, and spirit.

**Meditation:** In the final days of the Easter season, the Scripture readings challenge us to embrace the life and love of Jesus so that the Easter event becomes an Easter mentality that lasts year-round. We recognize that disciples of Jesus are to love as Jesus loved, translating our words and desires into action, always conscious that loving actions demonstrate the power of good over evil, and life over death.

**Prayer:** Spirit of the Living God, refresh us. May our leaders love you and tend your sheep, and may we accept our share of that responsibility as well.

## Bearing Witness

**Readings:** Acts 28:16-20, 30-31; John 21:20-25

**Scripture:**
There are also many other things that Jesus did, but if these were to be described individually, I do not think the whole world would contain the books that would be written. (John 21:25)

**Reflection:** If you've ever tried to tell the story of a grandparent or other family member to the next generation, you know how difficult it is to capture the essence of that person. What stories will communicate her humor? How will you explain her background or upbringing? What memories could help a new generation connect to her? And what about the experiences of other family members—how will you include their stories and memories? Of course, what you include also depends on what you are trying to achieve. Do you want them to grow to love her or simply be informed about her? It's a challenging task, isn't it?

Now imagine those same questions and concerns as they apply to passing on the story of Jesus. In the earliest days of preaching about Jesus, the intent was clear—the evangelists were not interested in creating a biography of a fascinating person. Instead, they wanted to ignite the flame of faith and hope that would draw their listeners and readers into a relationship with Jesus. And so, from among all the things they witnessed, they chose stories that would effectively communicate not just who Jesus was but why he matters.

The Gospels bear witness to the Son of God who is also one of us. They testify to the truth and goodness of God, as well as the justice and mercy necessary to form and sustain communities. The evangelists provide enough to draw us in and ignite our faith. Now it's up to us to discover how God is still acting through Jesus to create and sustain a lifelong relationship.

**Meditation:** Make it a practice to review your life as a follower of Christ. Which stories from the Scriptures have spoken most clearly to you in various periods? What might you want others to know about your own encounters with Jesus, or lessons you have learned along the way?

**Prayer:** Spirit of the Living God, refresh us. Allow us to discover the Good News of Jesus still alive in our midst, still too vast to contain, and still being told in the sacred testimony of our lives.

*June 8: Pentecost Sunday*

## Amending the Soil

**Readings:** Acts 2:1-11; 1 Cor 12:3b-7, 12-13 or Rom 8:8-17; John 20:19-23 or 14:15-16, 23b-26

**Scripture:**
Lord, send out your Spirit, and renew the face of the earth. (Ps 104:30)

**Reflection:** Our faces often reveal what is going on inside of us physically, mentally, and spiritually. What does the face of the earth reveal when beauty and serenity live side by side with pollution and battlegrounds? Or when creativity and care for the common good are being outpaced by sterile conformity and selfish hoarding? Oh, our earth could use some restoration for sure! While we cannot return to the idyllic Eden of the creation accounts, we can invite God's Spirit to help us be part of the renewal that's so desperately needed.

The same Spirit or breath of God that hovered over the earth's chaos in the first account of creation hovers over us still. We see evidence in its fruit, which Paul describes to the Galatians as love, joy, peace, patience, kindness, generosity, faithfulness, gentleness, and self-control (Gal 5:22-23). If we could pull back the surface of what is happening on our planet, would we find those virtues, or would we find rivalry, jealousy, envy, immorality, self-centeredness? We know that what lies beneath the surface feeds what grows on top of it.

The Spirit will help us amend the soil beneath the chaos if we're also willing to do some of the work of tilling and fertilizing and planting. What might that look like? Attending to the needs of the sick, respectfully engaging with people who are different from us, refusing to give in to revenge, learning to limit our over-consumption of goods, standing with those who are treated unjustly, giving and receiving forgiveness—these are just some of the things that make of our lives the healthy soil that will produce good fruit.

**Meditation:** We are often overwhelmed by the enormity of the world's ills and the volume of hateful noise that surrounds us. Instead, on this day when we celebrate the Spirit's presence among us, ask the Spirit to overwhelm you with compassion, strength of purpose, resilience, and hope. Make time for the stillness of prayer which will orient you to God's purposes.

**Prayer:** Spirit of the Living God, refresh us. Multiply our efforts to be part of restoring the beauty of the earth by caring for one another and embracing your vision for our existence.

# References

*Introduction*
*Abraham Joshua Heschel: Essential Writings*, ed. Susannah Heschel, Modern Spiritual Masters Series (Maryknoll, NY: Orbis Books, 2011).

*April 24: Thursday within the Octave of Easter*
The story behind the lyrics to "It Is Well with My Soul" may be found using a simple internet search. One such website is staugustine.com in an article dated October 16, 2014.

*April 25: Friday within the Octave of Easter*
G. K. Chesterton's book *Orthodoxy* was first published in England in 1908. His observation about the familiar and unfamiliar is found in chapter 1.

*May 9: Friday of the Third Week of Easter*
Thomas Aquinas on humility may be found in *Summa Theologica*, 161 (written in the late thirteenth century).

*May 10: Saturday of the Third Week of Easter*
"Our choice about who or what to follow, who or what to love, will determine everything" is inspired by the writings of Pedro Arrupe, SJ, missionary to Japan, and twenty-eighth superior general of the Society of Jesus.

*May 14: Saint Matthias*
Tertullian of Carthage is credited with writing the second-century work *Apologeticus*.

*May 21: Wednesday of the Fifth Week of Easter*
Macrina Wiederkehr, *Abide: Keeping Vigil with the Word of God* (Collegeville, MN: Liturgical Press, 2011).

*May 22: Thursday of the Fifth Week of Easter*
Henri Nouwen, *You Are the Beloved: Daily Meditations for Spiritual Living*, ed. Gabrielle Earnshaw (Colorado Springs: Convergent Books, 2017).
Dorothy Day, *The Duty of Delight: The Diaries of Dorothy Day*, ed. Robert Ellsberg (Milwaukee: Marquette University Press, 2008).

*May 29: Thursday of the Sixth Week of Easter*
Walter Brueggemann, *Praying the Psalms: Engaging Scripture and the Life of the Spirit*, 2nd ed. (Eugene, OR: Cascade Books, 2007).